One Little Goat

A PASSOVER SONG

One Little Goat

A PASSOVER SONG

adapted and illustrated by

MARILYN HIRSH

Holiday House
New York

Library of Congress Cataloging in Publication Data

Jews. Liturgy and ritual.
  [Had gadya. English]
  One little goat, a passover song.

  Translation of Had gadya.
  SUMMARY: After a little goat is eaten by a cat,
trouble cumulates until the Holy One puts things right.
The song is sung at the end of the seder on Passover.
  [1. Song, Jewish. 2. Passover] I. Hirsh, Marilyn.
II. Title.
BM670.H28H57   1979   296.4'37   78-24354
ISBN 0-8234-0345-9

In memory of the seders of my childhood.

One little goat, one little goat,
My father bought for two *zuzim*.*

*Old coins.

One little goat, one little goat.

Then came the cat and ate the goat,
My father bought for two *zuzim*.

One little goat, one little goat.

Then came the dog and bit the cat,
That ate the goat,

My father bought for two *zuzim*.
One little goat, one little goat.

Then came the stick and beat the dog,
That bit the cat, that ate the goat,

My father bought for two *zuzim*.
One little goat, one little goat.

Then came the fire and burned the stick,
That beat the dog, that bit the cat,
That ate the goat,

My father bought for two *zuzim*.
One little goat, one little goat.

Then came the water and put out the fire,
That burned the stick, that beat the dog,
That bit the cat, that ate the goat,

My father bought for two *zuzim*.
One little goat, one little goat.

Then came the ox and drank the water,
That put out the fire, that burned the stick,
That beat the dog, that bit the cat,

That ate the goat,
My father bought for two *zuzim*.
One little goat, one little goat.

Then came the butcher and butchered the ox,
That drank the water, that put out the fire,
That burned the stick, that beat the dog,

That bit the cat, that ate the goat,
My father bought for two *zuzim*.
One little goat, one little goat.

Then came the Angel of Death,
   and killed the butcher,
Who butchered the ox, that drank the water,
That put out the fire, that burned the stick,

That beat the dog, that bit the cat,
That ate the goat,
My father bought for two *zuzim*.
One little goat, one little goat.

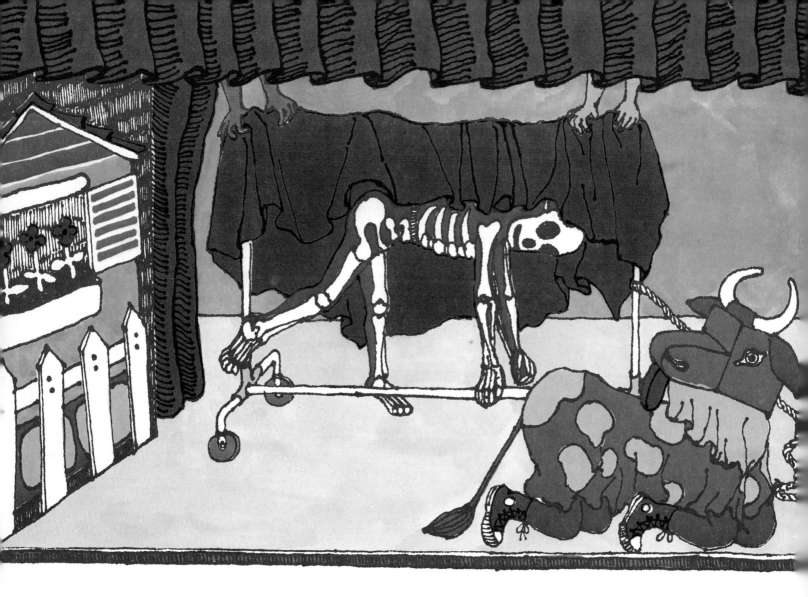

Then came the Holy One, blessed be He,
  and slew the Angel of Death,
Who killed the butcher, who butchered the ox,
That drank the water, that put out the fire,

That burned the stick, that beat the dog,
That bit the cat, that ate the goat,
My father bought for two *zuzim*.
One little goat, one little goat.

THE END

ONE LITTLE GOAT

1. One lit - tle goat,_____ one lit - tle goat, my_

Chorus begins

Chorus ends

fa - ther bought for_ two_ zu - zim. One lit - tle goat,_____ one lit - tle goat.

2. Then_ came the cat and ate_ the_ goat, my_

(Chorus)

fa - ther bought for_ two_ zu - zim. One lit - tle goat,_____ one lit - tle goat.

3. Then— came the dog and bit— the— cat, that— ate the goat, my—

(Chorus)

fa - ther bought for— two— zu - zim. One lit - tle goat,——— one lit - tle goat.

4. Then— came the stick and beat— the— dog, that—

Repeat these 2 phrases alternately, as many times as needed to finish each verse.

bit the cat, that— ate the goat, my— *(Chorus)*

ABOUT PASSOVER

"One Little Goat" is sung on Passover, the Jewish holiday of freedom. It celebrates the ancient story of Moses leading the Israelites out of Egypt, where they were forced to be slaves. Moses asked Pharaoh, Egypt's ruler, ten different times to free the Israelites. Each time, Pharaoh refused and each time, in order to convince him, God sent a plague on the Egyptian people. Pharaoh finally agreed after the tenth and worst plague, in which God sent the Angel of Death to slay the firstborn son in every Egyptian home. The Angel of Death "passed over" the homes of the Israelites, which is how the holiday got its name. On Passover, Jews do not rejoice in the sufferings of their enemies but give thanks instead for their own freedom. This holiday also celebrates the coming of spring.

Passover lasts for eight days. Traditionally, on the first two nights, family and guests gather around the dinner table for the *seder*. The *seder* is a service and meal that celebrates the historic event of the Israelites' departure from Egypt.

Everyone has a small book called a *Haggadah*, which explains the Passover story and the meaning of the special foods on the table. Each person reads from the *Haggadah* in turn. During the service, the youngest child asks four special questions, three of which are about some of the food on the table. Why does everyone eat *matzoh?* Why does everyone eat bitter herbs? Why is food being dipped in salt water? Why is everyone reclining? The answers become clear as the Passover story, stressing the suffering of the Israelite slaves and the joys of freedom, continues to be read. The *matzoh,* a flat bread, is a reminder that when Pharaoh finally let the slaves go, they had to leave Egypt so quickly that their bread dough didn't have time to rise. The bitter herbs recall the bitter suffering of the slaves, and the salt water is like the salty tears they shed. The reclining position in which everyone is sitting is like the position free men used during meals in ancient times.

In the middle of the *seder* service, a delicious dinner is served, which is different from the special Passover food already on the table. After dinner, more of the story is read, and songs are sung. The door is opened to welcome the prophet Elijah, who takes an invisible sip from a wine cup set aside for him. The very last song sung at the *seder* is *Had Gadya,* "One Little Goat."

ABOUT THE SONG

"One Little Goat" has a lively tune. By the time the *seder* is over, children are drowsy, and some of the littlest ones have fallen asleep. But this song is so much fun to sing that every child wakes up.

"One Little Goat" is a very old song. Printed copies of it exist in sixteenth-century *Haggadahs,* but it is probably even older. It was originally written in Aramaic, the language spoken by the ancient Jews. Some people think that the problems of the little goat stand for the history of the Jewish people, each character in the song being some nation that has tried to harm them. For example, the stick stands for Persia and the water for Rome. The happy ending shows that the Jews believe the Holy One will triumph over all evil. Folklore experts have found German and Persian songs that are not very different from "One Little Goat."

I have liked this song since I was a child, and I hope children will enjoy seeing it put on as a play. M.H.